SPACE

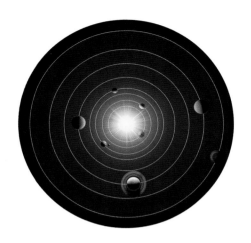

OUR SUN

Ian Graham

A+
Smart Apple Media

Published by Smart Apple Media,
an imprint of Black Rabbit Books
P.O. Box 3263, Mankato, Minnesota, 56002
www.blackrabbitbooks.com

Designed by Guy Callaby
Edited by Mary-Jane Wilkins

Cataloging-in-Publication Data is available
from the Library of Congress

ISBN 978-1-62588-210-3

Picture acknowledgements
t = top, b = bottom, l = left, r = right
title page De Mango; 2-3 Vadim Sadovski/
both Shutterstock; 4 Ryan Warnick/
Thinkstock; 5 Triff; 6 clearviewstock/both
Shutterstock; 7 NASA/JPL-Caltech/T. Pyle;
9 MarcelClemens; 10 Corepics VOF/both
Shutterstock; 11 NASA/JPL-Caltech;
12 solarseven; 13 ESA; 14 Alex Hubenov;
15 Denis Tabler; 16 Fisherss/all
Shutterstock; 17 Ints Vikmanis/Thinkstock;
18 Aptyp_koK/Shutterstock; 19 Rachel
Sanderoff/Thinkstock; 20 LingHK/
Shutterstock; 21 NASA Cover James Thew/
Thinkstock

Printed in China

DAD0057
032014
9 8 7 6 5 4 3 2 1

CONTENTS

OUR SUN

The Sun is a star like the thousands of other stars in the sky. It looks bigger and brighter than all the others because it is so much closer.

Uranus
Neptune
Jupiter
Earth
Mars
Saturn
Venus
Mercury
Sun

SUN'S GRAVITY

Earth's gravity pulls you down to the ground. The Sun's gravity is so strong that it holds the whole solar system together. Without the Sun, the planets would all fly away.

The Sun holds eight planets in orbit around it.

HOW FAR?

The Sun is 93 million miles (150 million km) away from us. An airplane would take about 19 years to fly the same distance!

The Sun spins around once every 25 days.

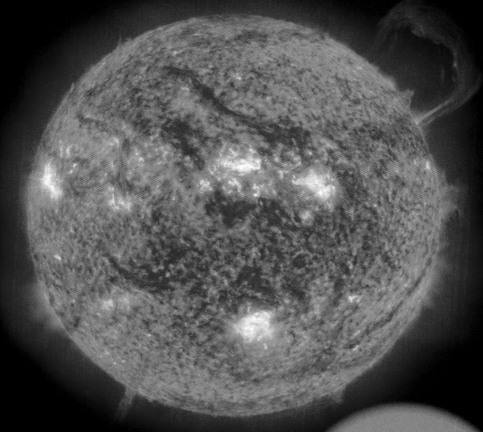

WARNING!

Never ever look at the Sun. The light and heat coming from the Sun are so strong that they would damage your eyes, maybe even causing blindness.

HOW BIG?

The Sun looks small in the sky, but it is a giant. It is so big that more than a million Earths would fit inside it.

SPOTLIGHT ON SPACE

MAKING A SUN

To make a Sun, you first need a vast cloud of gas and dust in space. Then an old star explodes nearby and gravity does the rest.

GAS AND DUST

The exploding star squashes the cloud. Then the cloud's own gravity begins to pull the gas and dust together. It makes a big ball in the middle that will become the Sun.

The Sun was born in a giant cloud of gas and dust like this.

NUCLEAR POWER

Stars like the Sun shine because of nuclear reactions going on deep inside them. The Sun works like a giant nuclear power station in space.

LIGHTING UP

At first, the Sun was just a ball of gas. As it grew bigger it also got hotter and hotter, until it suddenly burst into light and became a star.

The new Sun was surrounded by gas and dust that would become the planets.

INSIDE THE SUN

Scientists have figured out what is happening inside the Sun even though they can't see inside it or send space probes into it.

LIGHT AND HEAT

In the middle of the Sun, particles of matter crash into each other and stick together. It's called nuclear fusion and it produces the light and heat the Sun gives out.

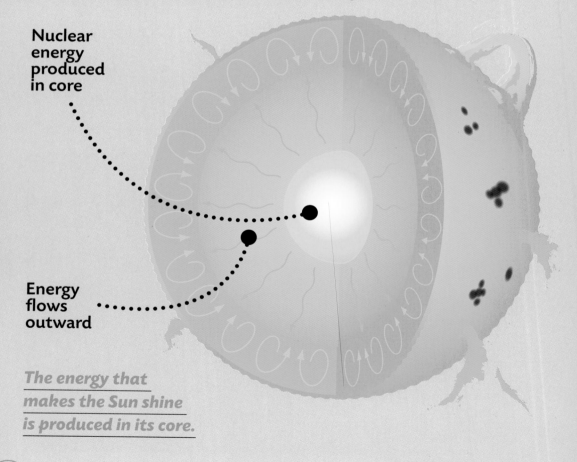

Nuclear energy produced in core

Energy flows outward

The energy that makes the Sun shine is produced in its core.

SUNSPOTS

Dark spots sometimes appear on the Sun. They are places where twists in the Sun's magnetic field stop hot gas rising to the surface for a while.

THE SUN'S ENERGY

It can take hundreds of thousands of years for energy to travel from the Sun's core to its surface. From there, it takes just over eight minutes to reach Earth.

Most sunspots disappear after one or two weeks.

THE SOLAR WIND

Particles of matter fly away from the Sun in all directions. This flow of particles is called the solar wind.

LIGHT IN THE SKY

When solar wind particles reach Earth, they dive into our atmosphere near the North and South Poles. They make the air glow. This glow in the sky is called an aurora.

An aurora like this, near the North Pole, is also called the Northern Lights.

WIND MACHINE

A spacecraft called *Genesis* was sent on a mission to collect solar wind particles. It spent more than two years in space gathering particles, and then brought them back to Earth.

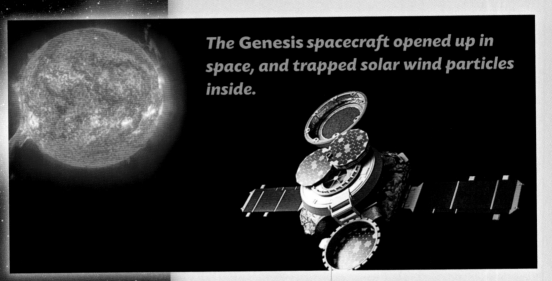

The Genesis spacecraft opened up in space, and trapped solar wind particles inside.

A SPEEDY WIND

The fastest particles of the solar wind speed through space at about 620 miles (1,000 km) a second. At this speed, you could travel around the world in only 40 seconds.

SPOTLIGHT ON SPACE

11

Storms on the Sun

The Sun looks like a calm yellow ball, but if you could see it up close it would look very different. Storms and explosions rage across the Sun's boiling surface.

Streamers of gas

Storms on the Sun hurl vast streamers of glowing gas out into space. Often, the gas falls back onto the Sun, but sometimes it is flung away across the solar system.

SOLAR SPACECRAFT

A spacecraft called the *Solar and Heliospheric Observatory (SOHO)* has been studying the Sun since 1996. It can give an early warning of storms on the Sun that might affect Earth.

*The **SOHO** spacecraft keeps a constant watch on the Sun.*

SPACE WEATHER

Gas flung out into space by the Sun can go in any direction. If it travels in our direction, it can damage satellites in orbit and cause power cuts.

SPOTLIGHT ON SPACE

Tongues of gas bigger than the Earth burst out of the Sun's surface.

Cosmic clock

People have used the seasons and the rising and setting of the Sun like calendars and clocks to measure the passing of time for thousands of years.

Shadow clocks

A sundial uses a shadow to tell the time. As the Sun crosses the sky, the shadow it casts on the sundial moves. To tell the time, see where the shadow points.

The Sun casts a shadow on a sundial with numbers showing the hours.

THE SPINNING EARTH

The Sun crosses the sky each day, but it isn't the Sun that is moving —it's the Earth. The Earth spins around once every 24 hours.

THE SEASONS

Earth tilts as it travels around the Sun. The part that tilts toward the Sun is warm—it's spring and summer there. The part that tilts away is colder, creating autumn and winter.

SPOTLIGHT ON SPACE

As Earth turns, the Sun rises in the east and crosses the sky

LIFE ON EARTH

Earth is the only planet where we know life exists. The Sun provides two things needed for life—warmth and light. Earth supplies the other two —water and oxygen.

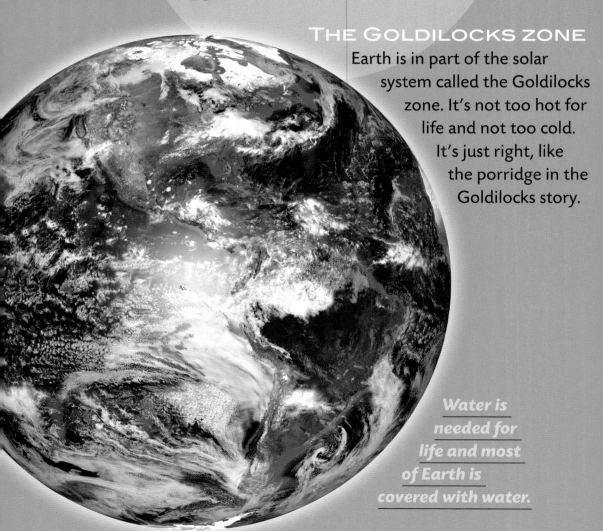

THE GOLDILOCKS ZONE

Earth is in part of the solar system called the Goldilocks zone. It's not too hot for life and not too cold. It's just right, like the porridge in the Goldilocks story.

Water is needed for life and most of Earth is covered with water.

Energy from the Sun

Green plants use the energy in sunlight for growth. We can't use energy straight from the Sun, but we can get it by eating plants, or by eating animals that have eaten plants.

Farms grow crops that convert energy from the Sun into food.

SOLAR POWERHOUSE

Every hour, Earth receives enough energy from the Sun to supply everyone in the world with all the energy they need for a year.

SPOTLIGHT ON SPACE

ECLIPSES

The Sun, Earth, and Moon sometimes line up together in space. The result is a spectacular event called an eclipse.

PARTIAL SOLAR ECLIPSE

During a partial solar eclipse, the Moon is not exactly in line with the Sun and Earth. It covers part of the Sun, which looks as if a bite has been taken out of it.

There are more partial solar eclipses than total solar eclipses.

During a total solar eclipse, the Sun's atmosphere becomes visible.

TOTAL SOLAR ECLIPSE

The Moon is 400 times smaller than the Sun. It's also 400 times closer than the Sun, so the tiny Moon can blot out the giant Sun. This is a total solar eclipse.

LUNAR ECLIPSE

Another type of eclipse happens when the Earth moves between the Sun and Moon, casting its shadow on the Moon. This is a lunar eclipse.

SPOTLIGHT ON SPACE

THE SUN'S FUTURE

The Sun will not last forever. One day in the far future it will run out of the hydrogen fuel that makes it shine and it will change in a big way.

THE SUN'S DEATH

When the Sun's core stops producing heat, the Sun will grow into a huge star called a red giant. Earth will probably be swallowed up by the giant dying star.

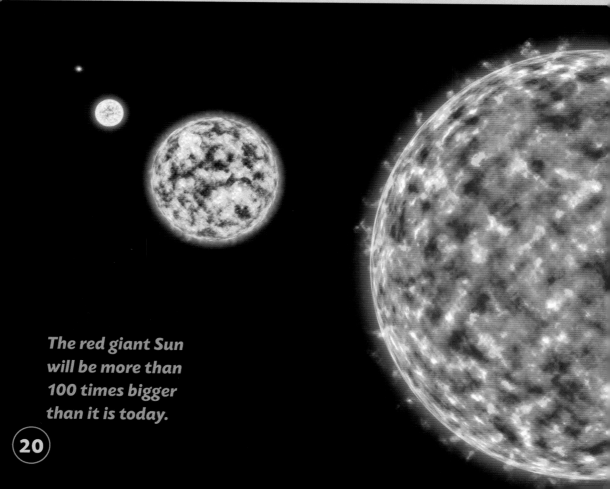

The red giant Sun will be more than 100 times bigger than it is today.

WHITE DWARF

A red giant blows its outer layers of gas away into space, leaving a tiny dim star called a white dwarf. Then the white dwarf Sun will slowly fade away.

This tiny dot is a white dwarf star left behind by a red giant.

WHEN WILL THE SUN DIE?

The Sun will go on shining as it does now for another five billion years before it begins to swell up and become a red giant.

SPOTLIGHT ON SPACE

GLOSSARY

atmosphere The gases that surround a star, planet, or moon.

aurora A shimmering glow in the sky near the north and south poles caused by the solar wind diving into the atmosphere.

billion A thousand million.

Earth The planet we live on, the third planet from the Sun.

eclipse An eclipse happens when an object in the sky passes in front of another one, hiding it from view.

Goldilocks zone The part of the solar system that is just the right distance from the Sun for liquid water to exist on a planet's surface, making life possible.

gravity The invisible force that pulls things toward a star, planet, moon or other large object and holds the solar system together.

hydrogen A gas; the Sun is made mostly of hydrogen.

magnetic field A place where magnetic forces exist.

moon A small world orbiting a larger object such as a planet.

nuclear reaction A process that makes energy by breaking apart the centers of big atoms or by crashing the centers of small atoms together.

observatory A building or spacecraft that studies events and objects in space.

orbit The path of a planet, spacecraft, or moon around a larger body.

oxygen A gas in Earth's atmosphere that living creatures breathe.

planet A large world in orbit around the Sun or another star.

red giant A huge star that has swollen up because it is running out of fuel.

seasons Times of the year with different weather—spring, summer, autumn, and winter.

solar To do with the Sun. Solar energy is the energy in sunlight.

solar system The Sun and all the planets, moons, and other bodies that travel through space with it.

solar wind Particles that travel away from the Sun in all directions.

Sun The star at the center of the solar system.

sundial A device that shows the time by a shadow cast by the Sun.

WEB SITES

http://www.nasa.gov/vision/universe/solarsystem/sun_for_kids_main.html
Find out why we study the Sun from the space agency, NASA.

http://imagine.gsfc.nasa.gov/docs/science/know_l1/dwarfs.html
Read about white dwarf stars.

http://www.sciencekids.co.nz/sciencefacts/space/sun.html
Lots of interesting facts about the Sun.

http://www.howstuffworks.com/sun.htm
See how the Sun works.

http://science.howstuffworks.com/nature/climate-weather/atmospheric/question471.htm
Learn more about auroras and how the Sun causes them.

http://www.enchantedlearning.com/subjects/astronomy/stars/fusion.shtml
Learn more about nuclear fusion, the process that makes the Sun shine so brightly.

http://www.esa.int/esaKIDSen/SEMGO5WJD1E_OurUniverse_0.html
Read about eclipses, from the European Space Agency (ESA).

INDEX